THE
CRABB FAMILY
COLLECTION

Cover Photo: John Bowen

ISBN 978-1-4950-9332-6

HAL•LEONARD®
7777 W. BLUEMOUND RD. P.O. BOX 13819 MILWAUKEE, WI 53213

Visit Hal Leonard Online at
www.halleonard.com

THE CROSS

Words and Music by
GERALD CRABB

To some it's just __ an em - blem, a for -
see why this __ old em - blem is so

cross made for the Son of God __ at Cal - va - ry, __ two

piec - es of __ rough tim - ber on __ a hill. __ Through His

hands and through __ His feet, __ He took the nails for you and __ me.

An - gels watched as He died __ for the lost. Though He

GOOD DAY

Words and Music by
GERALD CRABB

DON'T YOU WANNA GO

Words and Music by
GERALD CRABB

Bluegrass feel, in 2

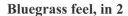

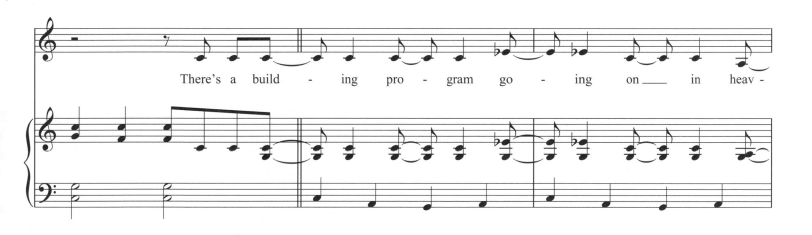

There's a build - ing pro - gram go - ing on ___ in heav -

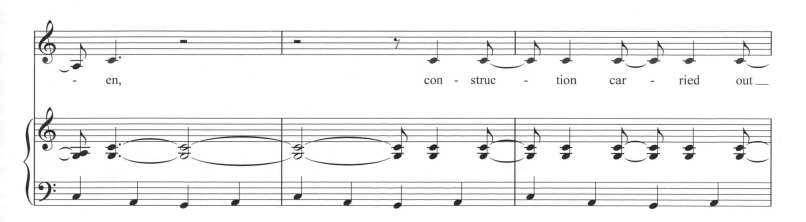

- en, con - struc - tion car - ried out ___

HE CAME LOOKING FOR ME

Words and Music by
GERALD CRABB

PLEASE COME DOWN TO ME

Words and Music by
GERALD CRABB

know that there __ are oth - ers who could of - fer more __ than I. __

I prom - ise You __ I'd un - der - stand

if for me You had __ no time. I

think I just __ hit bot - tom, __ and I'm look - ing up to see. __

HE'LL MAKE A WAY

Words and Music by
GERALD CRABB

Easy Bluegrass feel

Look-ing for an-swers, _ you need a way
Red Sea, _ and no place to

out. _
go. _

You've been trapped in that
Phar-aoh's ar-my was

tri-al, _ full of sor-row and doubt. _
clos-ing in; they'd soon o-ver-throw. _

PLEASE FORGIVE ME

Words and Music by
GERALD CRABB

oth-ers find __ the way. __ At Your mer - cy, please __ for -

give me.

All I have __ is You. __ Ooh. _____

THE REASON THAT I'M STANDING

Words and Music by GERALD CRABB
and C. AARON WILBURN

man-y times ___ I have re-called the Sav - ior's words, _ so true: _ "If
you won't be ___ a-shamed _ of Me, _ I ___ won't be ___ of you." _ So I'll ___
proud - ly stand un - til ___ I see ___ the
face of ___ the One ___ who gave _ ev-'ry-thing _ for _ me. When the

The road has not __ been eas - y; at times I've lost __ my way. __ So of - ten I __ have stum - bled, search - ing for the light __ of day. __ Cir - cum-

THAT'S NO MOUNTAIN

Words and Music by
GERALD CRABB

Slow Gospel feel

I looked at that moun-tain __ that stood in my way. Would

this be my last __ climb? Could this be my fate? __ And my

heart beat __ so fear-ful; __ what chal-lenge a - waits? But

THROUGH THE FIRE

Words and Music by
GERALD CRABB

show up, yes, ___ and He will take you through the fire ___ a - gain. ___

___ I know with - in ___ my - self ___ that ___

___ I ___ would sure - ly per - ish. Oh, but if I trust ___ the might - y hand of God, He'll

shield the flames ___ a - gain, ___ a - gain. ___

THE WALK

Words and Music by
GERALD CRABB

Moderately, with energy

I found my-self seat-ed in the line __ of fire. __ That old preach-er man __ sure had the ho- -ly pow'r. __ With his Bi-ble, he __ read my __ life like he knew

Male vocal written at sung pitch.

To Coda

lot I can't __ re- call. _____ But I won't for- get __ the mer- cy and I won't __

__ for- get __ the walk. _____ As he

o- pened up __ the hymn- book and be- gan _____ to sing, _____ a

cloud of joy __ filled the build- ing like __ a cov- er- ing. __ "With the in-

THE SHEPHERD'S CALL

Words and Music by
GERALD CRABB